RANDOM HOUSE AUSTRALIA
❖ GUIDES TO GARDEN DESIGN ❖

Herb & Kitchen Garden

RANDOM HOUSE AUSTRALIA
GUIDES TO
✧ GARDEN DESIGN ✧

Herb &
Kitchen
Garden

✧ A. M. CLEVELY ✧

RANDOM HOUSE
A U S T R A L I A

Random House Australia Pty Ltd
20 Alfred Street, Milsons Point NSW 2061

Sydney   New York   Toronto
London   Auckland
and agencies throughout the world

First published in Australia in 1993

Edited, designed and produced by
Robert Ditchfield Ltd
Combe Court
Kerry's Gate
Hereford HR2 0AH

ISBN 0 09 182785 X

Typeset in Great Britain by Action Typesetting Ltd, Gloucester
Printed and bound in Belgium

ACKNOWLEDGEMENTS

Photographs are reproduced by kind permission of the following: Robert Ditchfield
Ltd (photographer Bob Gibbons) 22 and (photographer Jerry Hardman-Jones) 25;
Thompson & Morgan: 41. All other photographs are by Diana Saville who would like
to thank the owners of the gardens which include Barnsley House (16, 32, 39),
Batemans (57), Bourton House (1, 19 below, 33, 61), Close Farm (12), Eastgrove
Cottage Garden (11), Elm Close (6), Glenmore Park (50), Hergest Croft (18/19, 35, 36,
54, 59), Hill Court (31), Lower Hope (53), Misarden (38), The Neuadd (13, 60),
Pentwyn Cottage (45), Preen Manor (15, 21 below, 26, 30, 34, 37, 48, 55),
Springfield Bungalow (10, 49), Stone Cottage (46 right), Rotherwas (50), Torwood
(56/57), Westbury Court Garden (40), Woodlands (cover, 5, 7, 8/9, 14, 21 above, 29,
42, 47), Woodpeckers (2, 16/17, 27), Yew Tree Cottage (24).

ILLUSTRATIONS

Page 1: Tiny box-hedged potager.
Frontispiece: Cordon apples over an arch.
Page 5: Ornamental cabbages.

CONTENTS

INTRODUCTION

The first gardens were essentially practical, created from necessity and devoted to the cultivation of useful plants. Whether grown for food or as sources of condiments, dyes, medicinal remedies and perfumes, much of this early flora is still planted and tended today, even though selected and developed in some cases almost beyond recognition.

ABOVE: *Traditional vegetable garden (with cat) laid out in calm rows; spires of gladioli are in the foreground.*
OPPOSITE: *A perfectly arranged potager that combines flowers and vegetables.*

The value and fascination of these plants is perennial, but modern gardeners intending to grow herbs, fruit and vegetables have a distinct advantage over their predecessors. Choice rather than necessity motivates our decision, and whereas a garden would once evolve around the production of food, useful plants are now expected to blend into an overall design as just one of several satisfying visual elements.

Utility crops have aesthetic qualities too, often overlooked during the more prosaic business of growing them to use. Their leaf shapes and colours rival those of more familiar foliage plants, many have attractive and sometimes edible flowers, while their variety of form extends from the prostrate to the architecturally dominating.

By reviving ancient skills of training and pruning, many herbs, fruit and even vegetable crops can be manipulated into sculptural and decorative shapes. Because of the necessity for access to plant, cultivate and harvest, even the basic layout of herb and kitchen gardens offers opportunities for unique visual geometries.

The essayist Joseph Addison wrote: 'I have always thought a kitchen garden a more pleasant sight than the finest orangery'. With flair and careful planning, beauty can be combined with utility, so that the productive garden also becomes an ornamental garden in its own right.

Surrounding and defining a garden with fences, hedges or walls is something we take for granted, but enclosure was a relatively novel concept in the Middle Ages. Contemporary illustrations and embroideries show for the first time recognizable gardens contained within high walls, so transforming a mere cultivated plot into a private place for contemplation and diversion.

Chiefly herbs and fruit were grown, for the appreciation of green vegetables was still in its infancy. Arbours, seats and pergolas were important features of the medieval garden, with small simple beds laid in deliberately symmetrical patterns. The design of herb and kitchen gardens still depends on these timeless elements.

In the sixteenth century garden design rapidly became more sophisticated, imitating the elaborate and ornamental traditions of tapestry, embroidery and heraldry. From complex rectangular patterns of paths and walkways dividing small beds, each often containing a

single kind of plant, evolved the intricate and formal designs that characterize knots and parterres. Dwarf hedges of box, rosemary, hyssop and lavender enclosed groups of herbs and vegetables, as in the restored potager at Villandry.

During the more turbulent periods of European history, gardening skills and traditions were kept alive by the monasteries. There the need for contemplation and self-sufficiency produced functional garden sanctuaries: the herbularius (physic garden) with its collection of aromatic and medicinal herbs, for example, and the equally essential hortus (vegetable garden). Plans for monasteries such as that at Turin in 1607 show aesthetically neat gardens in which hermits could work and pray. Maximum efficiency went hand in hand with beauty.

The growing wealth of landowners in the sixteenth and seventeenth centuries resulted in grandiose formal kitchen gardens, which tended to be banished from sight as the Landscape Movement increasingly demanded lavish vistas and fine views. Grand estates with large households required vast supplies of fruit, herbs and vegetables, and kitchen gardens expanded to cope with this insatiable demand.

The popular habit of

A highly formal parterre organized through the means of slim brick paths and the geometric lines of box hedging.

They still influence design principles for gardeners with much less ground at their disposal. The impact of these gardens, however, depends on their expansive scale, and attempts to re-create them in miniature in smaller gardens seldom succeed. They provide a qualified source of ideas for garden design, their unique value lying not in their scale or size, but in the wealth of ideas and skills displayed for tending plants, together with the diversity of crops grown.

During the age of great plant hunters and overseas exploration, the range of cultivated plants rapidly increased. Classic kitchen gardens came to include numerous crops less commonly seen today. They deserve revival, both for ornament and nutritional variety. Artichokes, seakale, salsify and orach, weeping grapes and dwarf standard quinces, mop-head bays and mats of pennyroyal all have strategic places in the modern garden.

Vita Sackville-West enjoyed 'muddling up' attractive plants of all kinds in her gardens, herbs and vegetables side by side with flowers, while environmentally sensitive gardeners stress the importance of biodiversity. In cottage gardens these principles have been practised unconsciously for a century or more; rigid segregation of plants according to type makes little sense in small gardens.

The enduring charm of cottage gardens derives largely from this unorthodox mingling of plants and the imaginative use of space, but underlying the apparent artlessness is a refreshing way of valuing plants. Where food plants have equal status with ornamentals, they receive similar attention. Grown amongst flowers, as in the cottage garden, they are also seen to have an equivalent beauty, which ought to be taken into account when planning for utility crops.

Good kitchen and herb garden design, then, depends on more than the arrangement of layouts for maximum yield. The plants themselves are vital elements in the composition, offering as great a diversity of colour, shape and fragrance as any flower border.

How and where to use them to advantage in the garden is ultimately a matter for personal inclination, constrained by soil type, position and the amount of space available. By drawing on the several mainstream traditions, however, and experimenting with plant combinations and cultural techniques, it is possible to create a unique edible landscape that is at once productive and a joy to work and live in.

visiting stately homes on open days has fixed in the public mind this image of kitchen gardens measured by the acre, often sub-divided into manageable beds by low box hedges and enclosed by high walls that support decoratively trained fruit. Crops were planted in long, widely-spaced rows for easy maintenance, often by horse-drawn implements. Large herb gardens shared their impressive formality.

Ruby chard; its veins and stems are glowing red.

A NEW LOOK AT EDIBLE PLANTS

The most obvious appeal of cropping plants, even in a commercial or classic kitchen garden context, is to the gardener's instinct to control naturally wayward growth. Freshly earthed-up rows of potatoes, upright stands of peas, a strawed bed of flowering strawberries or neatly clipped rosemary hedges suggest reassuring discipline.

Rectangular vegetable beds echo this orderliness, essential where constant maintenance and easy access are prime considerations. Edible crops often grow quickly, faster than many flowers, for example, and need frequent attention. A formal layout makes this work easier to manage with minimal effort and distance to walk. Herb borders, too, can seem formless unless arranged in strong patterns.

Within these practical constraints, however, there is considerable room to manoeuvre and deploy striking arrangements that reveal the more subtle qualities of crop plants. A mature specimen of fennel, or parsley grown as continuous edging rival a delicate fernery; broad (fava) bean flowers emit a heady fragrance that the ancients thought would anaesthetize the unwary forever; artistically composed, the different coloured forms of chard or lettuce can resemble foliage bedding plants.

Shrewd choice of variety may enhance the decorative impact with unusual colours and forms, while even when past maturity many edible plants retain their design value. The drumstick seedheads of leeks are eagerly sought by flower arrangers, lettuce bolting to flower imitates conical topiary, and asparagus foliage or 'bower' in autumn is gloriously golden, studded with the scarlet berries of female plants.

Red sage (Salvia officinalis 'Purpurascens') is handsome enough to be grown in a border.

Colour

Although a familiar aspect of presentation at the table, the colour of vegetables is less usually considered as a garden design element, yet coloured forms of common plants can be employed as highlights or for contrast. Red and white bi-coloured runner (stick) beans, for example, golden marjoram and crimson-leafed grapes, variegated strawberries and horseradish, or purple-podded peas make these crops attractive features.

Red Plants

In many plants red pigments can dominate and so mask the normal green coloration. Red varieties of cabbage and Brussels sprouts turn green after cooking but have a brooding intensity during growth and often escape the attentions of birds. Purple-podded peas and beans are strikingly conspicuous against their green foliage and easy to locate for picking.

Combine herbs such as red sage, *Salvia officinalis* 'Purpurascens', and opal basil, *Ocimum basilicum purpureum*, with white or silver-leafed varieties for dramatic contrast.

Golden Plants

Whereas red plants recede from view in poor light, gold and silver-leafed varieties generate their own brilliance and are usually wasted in a brightly lit position. Cardoons, for example, need a dark green backdrop such as a yew hedge to enhance their majestic silver leaves.

Use these colours to illuminate darker surroundings, planting golden marjoram to edge dark paving, or yellow French (bush) bean varieties next to the rich green of spinach. Gold/green and white/green variegation are other useful colour highlights to attract attention or relieve a darker area, but avoid growing them in deep shade which may cause reversion to plain green.

LEFT: *Tall biennial angelica makes a stately flowering tower.*

however, have an overall form or leaf shape that is attractive, especially when planted in selected positions. Rhubarb becomes romantic beside a garden pool where its large spreading leaves shade pond fauna and contribute an almost tropical appearance. The succulent, densely sprawling stems of New Zealand spinach (*Tetragonia tetragonioides*) with leaves like rich green spear-heads make excellent ground cover, as does the less territorial asparagus pea (*Lotus tetragonolobus*) whose luxuriant foliage is constantly strewn with a combination of winged pods and vermilion flowers.

Using edible plants as sculptural components of a design might seem like aesthetic self-indulgence, for the serious business of growing crops rarely includes ornamental considerations. Observant gardeners soon discover, however, that yield and quality improve with thoughtful husbandry and attention to training. Courgettes (zucchini) grown as standards occupy little space and produce clean, easily accessible fruits; a fan-trained gooseberry fence bears the largest, earliest berries; clipping a rosemary hedge keeps growth satisfyingly dense with a bonus harvest of shoots for drying.

Form and Function

Pause for a moment to assess the shape of individual vegetables, fruits and herbs by the same criteria as any flowering tree, shrub or herbaceous plant. All herbs have decorative habits, from the towering exuberance of lovage and angelica down to prostrate mats of the tiny mint, *Mentha requienii.* Fruiting plants too have natural structural beauty or can be trained into satisfying patterns; mulberries, for example, grow into gnarled bizarre shapes like full-size bonsai, while a fan-trained pear on a house wall is equal to any decorative climber.

Some vegetables are less pleasing to look at than others, and such crops as potatoes and swedes (rutabaga) are difficult to use in landscape terms. Most,

Fragrance and Frivolity

Herbs are the supreme aromatic plants, notably when hot sunshine evaporates their essential oils on a still afternoon. Planted together their combined effect can be overpowering, even jarring, and the most fragrant herbs are best blended into any design as strategic plants to be appreciated individually. Grow them beside seats or where they are brushed in passing; prostrate herbs planted in paths surrender their scent when trodden upon.

Vegetables and fruits are less renowned for fragrance, although here too physical contact sometimes produces pleasant surprises. The subtle scent of parsnip foliage has a lingering sweetness many gardeners find irresistible, while black currant stems and leaves yield a pungent spiciness that has earned their use in perfume distilling.

Flowering plants have always been grown in kitchen gardens for ornament, cutting or as companion plants to deter pests and attract beneficial insects. Bees and insect predators such as hoverflies love the flowers of herbs and simple annuals like pot marigolds, poached-egg plant (*Limnanthes douglasii*) or dwarf morning glory, *Convolvulus minor*. Varieties of tagetes, on the other hand, have been found to protect neighbouring plants from insect pests.

Appreciating the various qualities and characteristics of cropping plants can inspire effective design ideas that help make the edible landscape satisfying on several levels. Trailing tomatoes can be used in window boxes and hanging baskets, grape vines as wall-coverings, low fruiting fences or weeping standards.

Outdoor cucumbers and marrows (summer squashes) train easily on trelliswork or bamboo cane teepees as lush climbers. Alternatively they will spread and root as moisture-retentive groundcover amongst sweet corn plants, which in turn can support climbing beans whose nitrogen-rich roots help sustain the other crops.

Aromatic and evergreen rosemary planted beside a seat can be sniffed all year round.

DESIGNING WITH CROP PLANTS

ABOVE: *Ornamental cabbages*
OPPOSITE: *This potager contains features to provide permanent vertical interest, like the clipped mop-head holly and the arches.*

While the design of kitchen and herb gardens should exploit the inherent qualities of the plants, whether visual, tactile or aromatic, it is important to remember that the main motive for growing them is their ultimate harvest and use. Curly kale and multi-coloured cabbages have sometimes been planted deliberately as seasonal bedding, a row of runner beans as a temporary screen to hide an eyesore, but cultivation is normally directed towards eventual consumption.

Balancing practicality with aesthetics is a nice art, and it is easy to exalt one above the other. If self-sufficiency in food crops or medicinal remedies is the sole motive, row-cropping with easy access for hoeing, weeding and thinning is the most utilitarian approach. Growing principles imitate those of the farmer, who prepares the soil, sows and cultivates, and finally clears the ground once more after harvesting his crop.

Most gardeners, however, prefer to grow a little of everything, gathering a wide variety of edible plants together in a cosmopolitan community. Their needs will differ considerably – some like rich living, others low fertility in scorching sunlight; peas and raspberries are usually grown in long lines, whereas short rows, square patches or individual sites are more appropriate for radishes, chervil or sweet corn.

Far from complicating matters, this cultural diversity actually aids imaginative design and helps demolish traditional barriers between productive and amenity gardening. Unlike a shrubbery or herbaceous border, the contents of a kitchen garden are always changing, and even a formal herb garden must make room for annual herbs. Only the framework of beds, paths and hedges remains fixed, within whose basic symmetry changing patterns and combinations appear seasonally.

Long-term Planting

Some vegetables, many herbs and most kinds of fruit are hardy perennials. Longevity, though, is relative. Rosemary will live for many years, whereas sage often needs renewal after three to four seasons; a pear tree will last a gardener's lifetime, asparagus beds thirty years or more, but a strawberry bed only three years before quality declines.

The layout of any herb or kitchen garden depends for continuity on the most durable perennials, especially evergreens, to provide boundaries, focal highlights and internal divisions. Hedges of dwarf box are traditional for edging kitchen garden beds, but other plants including evergreen herbs or low-espaliered fruit are alternatives. In the herb garden, geometrical arrangements of perennials such as artemisia, thyme, hyssop and germander create valuable year-round outlines.

Annual Change

The importance of a stimulating layout with permanent features is most obvious in winter when areas of soil are frequently bare. Mulching and the use of green manure cover-crops can reduce this stark contrast as well as improving the nature of the soil, but it is impossible to avoid the fact that successful harvests result in cleared ground, while even some perennials are deciduous and disappear in winter.

A conspicuous element of this seasonal change is a dramatic reduction in height. A kitchen garden in winter can resemble a ploughed field, the herb garden a diminished pattern of low mats and hummocks. While tall runner beans, artichokes, fennel and even rhubarb in flower lift the eye-line in summer, effective design depends for vertical interest out of season on taller shrubs and small trees – sweet bay or rosemary, for example, standard plants such as roses or red currants, and decoratively trained topfruit.

Rotations and Sequences

The cultivation of healthy vegetables depends on the principles of rotation. Changing cropping patterns so that a particular type of crop is not grown in the same piece of ground in consecutive years avoids the build-up of soil-borne pests and diseases and the depletion of essential nutrients. Three or four years is the usual interval before replanting an area with a crop of roots (carrots, parsnips, etc.), legumes (peas and beans) or brassicas (cabbage family).

Kitchen gardens were traditionally quartered with cruciform paths so that groups could circulate and return to their original sites every four years, but in smaller or irregularly shaped gardens crop rotation allows an infinite variety of annual design options.

ABOVE: *Small beds allow for easy crop rotation and some interplanting.*

RIGHT: *Flowering seakale (Crambe maritima) beside an old terracotta forcing jar; it is a connoisseur's crop which will rarely be found in a shop.*

Succession

For continuity of supply some vegetables are sown several times at regular intervals during a single season. Radishes and lettuces, for example, can be sown and cleared in about two months. Estimating how long plants occupy the ground is critical for the efficient use of space. In small beds assemble crops that mature and are cleared at the same time. Distinguish varieties which can be harvested over a long period from those that are cleared with a single picking as this will affect both the continuity and the appearance of the garden.

Experience will reveal unorthodox ways to save time and effort, although ensuring their success may affect seasonal planning. Chervil is a short-lived annual herb, but repeated sowings can be avoided by growing it in a permanent bed, encouraging plants to self-sow for succession. Parsley plants left to flower will of their own accord produce a generous bed of summer seedlings for transplanting elsewhere.

Discovering your Style

Before planning a productive garden or adapting an existing area to this end, try to assess its purpose together with your own priorities and resources. Even the simplest gardens need maintenance, with a regular input of time and stamina. A small garden of perennial herbs probably needs the least attention, a minimal amount of clipping, tidying and the occasional renewal of aging plants being sufficient to sustain an attractive and fragrant sanctuary.

Kitchen gardens are more demanding, depending on the proposed scale of operations. Self-sufficiency in food crops is difficult and onerous, most gardeners having neither the land nor the inclination to grow large quantities of staple crops such as maincrop potatoes, onions, winter carrots or cooking apples. Unless this is your aim,

concentrate instead on grow-ing the fruits and vegetables you like most, especially any seldom in shops or those best gathered fresh from the garden: leafy salads, sweet corn, gooseberries, white currants. Connoisseur crops such as golden raspberries, seakale, salsify and alpine strawberries are particularly suitable.

Explore alternative methods of cultivation that might make a virtue of small spaces, impoverished soils or simply lack of time. Deep vegetable beds are thoroughly prepared once every four to five years and then closely planted to suppress weeds and conserve moisture; if constructed about 4ft/1.2m wide there is no need to walk on the beds, which compacts the soil and so impedes growth and drainage.

Raised beds may bring the ground up to a more comfort-able working level and allow you to provide special soil conditions for plants that might not otherwise thrive – blueberries, for example, which need very acid soil. Herbs can be grown in orna-mental containers or as edgings for flower and veg-etable beds, a few fresh salad plants in a simple potager or integrated amongst her-baceous flowers.

PLANNING THE KITCHEN GARDEN

Plans that ignore the character of the soil are unlikely to succeed. Soil types vary widely, even within a single property, and few are immediately suitable for vegetable crops. Dig trial holes at intervals around the plot to identify the type and depth of soil, and to discover whether water drains away freely. A wet subsoil can indicate impeded drainage which will adversely affect plant growth, and any improvements should be made at a preliminary stage.

Test the soil for its pH status – its degree of acidity or alkalinity. Most vegetables prefer a neutral or slightly alkaline soil (pH 7.00 or above); adding lime makes acid soils more alkaline, while sulphur, ferrous sulphate and leafmould all increase acidity. Very light porous soils need fortifying with rotted manure, garden compost and other organic humus-forming materials. Sticky clay soils are made more manageable by the addition of coarse organic matter, or lime, or gypsum and dolomite (1 part: 4 parts) or by exposure to frost.

The lie of the land is important, too. Vegetables need plenty of light for healthy balanced growth, together with shelter from cold and destructive winds.

Hedges, fences and fruit trees make efficient shelter belts and windbreaks, but check they do not cast deep shade for more than half the day. Watch where sunlight falls around the garden and for how long, as this helps distinguish warmer and colder areas that may suit particular crops. Make sure the garden is not so enclosed that it becomes a frost trap in winter. Transform problem areas into assets: use a dark corner, for example, to house the compost heap, a steep sunny bank to force early sowings, a shady bed to protect mid-summer salads.

The amount of ground available will inevitably affect the design of the layout and the kind of crops grown. A plot 20ft/6m × 30ft/9m should supply all the summer vegetables for a family of four; twice this area will give plenty of produce for winter storage, excluding a bulk crop like maincrop potatoes. A salad garden, for raising lettuces, radishes, spring (salad) onions, beetroot and a few tomato plants perhaps, need occupy only a small border 3ft/90cm × 12ft/3.6m. Remember that tall plants such as runner beans, sweet corn or artichokes shade others nearby and therefore need more space than small plants harvested while young.

Paths

Adequate access is always essential, but depends on the kind of work undertaken. Brick paths 1ft/30cm wide are sufficient to divide beds in a small potager, 18in/45cm is more suitable between larger vegetable beds, while main paths should be at least 3ft/90cm wide to allow the comfortable passage of a wheelbarrow.

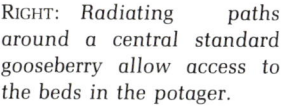

ABOVE: *Old bush apple trees, underplanted with polyanthus and bulbs, make a shelter belt around a kitchen garden.*

RIGHT: *Radiating paths around a central standard gooseberry allow access to the beds in the potager.*

Regular cultivation, especially in winter, transfers soil to paths, and they should therefore be easy to maintain. No paving material is ideal: bricks or blocks are attractive but must be laid firmly, especially on unstable soils; gravel is soon laid or levelled, but will host weeds; grass blends well, though it needs regular mowing and can invade adjacent beds; concrete is the most trouble-free, but visually unsatisfactory.

Supplies

Vegetable gardening depends on fertility. Chemical fertilizers on their own cannot sustain healthy soil nor the activity of its beneficial micro-organisms. Allocate an area for compost and manure. The former can be kept in neat bins or containers that accelerate decomposition, while manure stacked to rot can be planted with marrows, pumpkins or ridge cucumbers as a productive disguise.

Watering will usually be necessary at certain times of year, and in larger gardens can be supplied through pipework buried beneath paths and coupled to standpipes. Make sure plans allow for manoeuvring a hosepipe safely around beds where necessary.

Beds and Borders

Although the various cultural and harvesting requirements of vegetables are best served by growing in rows within a formal layout, beds need not be rectangular or even regular in shape and size. Plants such as aubergines (eggplants), tomatoes and courgettes are individuals; only a few may be needed and can be grown as specimens in corners, narrow borders or in the centre of beds. Even some crops normally grown in long rows – carrots, lettuce or peas, for example – will adapt to square blocks and broad drills a foot (30cm) or more wide.

Beds divided by paths are best kept below 5ft/1.4m wide to minimize trampling on the soil. Larger beds can be subdivided with temporary paths of shredded bark, spent hay, straw or even grass deliberately sown and then spaded off in autumn to stack as loam for potting compost. Rows of irregular length can be fitted into large beds by planting diagonally, or geometrical designs can be made by separating blocks of plants with outlines of lettuce or rows of peas.

The edges of beds are best kept neatly finished, either with hard materials such as a row of bricks or partly buried tiles, or with plants grown formally as a sheltering hedge and decorative margin. Narrow borders can be left between main beds and paths for use as seed and nursery beds, or to accommodate trained fruit and flowering plants, traditionally grown as decorative edgings.

Some plants for edges: alpine strawberries, bedding dahlias, blue grass (*Festuca glauca*), chives, cut-and-come-again lettuce, dwarf box, evergreen herbs, miniature roses, nasturtiums, parsley, pinks (dianthus) and sweet Williams for cutting.

Cropping Plans

Sketching on paper where each vegetable will be grown is a valuable preliminary way to avoid duplication, confusion and gaps in supply. Seed packets and handbooks often give estimated yields to help you plan quantities to sow. Start with well-known reliable varieties: later an alternative can be grown for comparison. Spread the work-load according to the season to prevent periods of hectic activity and a sudden glut of crops.

Sow and plant according to the weather, not the calendar. Precocious spring sowings before the soil is warm enough often fail, although glass cloches and handlights, some of them ornamental, will protect vulnerable crops. Find out when the last frosts normally occur locally, because tender plants such as runner beans, tomatoes and courgettes are not safe without protection until after this date. In cold gardens be prepared to cover vulnerable crops in the autumn, too, so extending the season at both ends.

As well as selecting tried varieties, make sure they are the right type for your needs. Maincrop carrots, for example, take two to three months longer to mature than short early varieties, and a

ABOVE: *Dwarf box gives a neat definition to the edges of beds.*
RIGHT: *Young sweet corn; this crop needs heat and full sun to thrive.*

trailing marrow fills a larger area of ground than a bush type. Varieties resistant to pests and diseases, drought or short day-length are indispensible for difficult conditions, while short-rooted types of carrots and similar crops are best for shallow soils.

EASILY-GROWN VEGETABLES
Broad and French beans, beetroot, carrots, chicory, courgettes and marrows, kale, loose-leaf lettuce, perpetual spinach, ridge cucumbers, Swiss chard, Welsh (perennial) onions.

GREATEST YIELD FOR THE LEAST EFFORT
Beetroot, carrots, courgettes, dwarf French beans, lettuce, tomatoes.

Sprinters and Stayers

Some vegetables take much longer than others to mature, while a few occupy the ground for a year or more. Sow those that sprint to a finish as fillers between slower-growing crops, clearing them promptly to allow the others to continue filling out.

Where a harvested crop leaves a bare space, make a further sowing straightaway or transplant seedlings waiting in a nursery bed. Most early vegetables are sprinters: you can

SPRINTERS		STAYERS	
French (bush) beans	10 weeks	Broad (fava) beans	20 weeks
Runner (stick) beans	10 weeks	Sprouting broccoli	40 weeks
Beetroot	12 weeks	Brussels sprouts	30 weeks
Chinese cabbage	10 weeks	Spring cabbage	32 weeks
Calabrese	12 weeks	Winter cabbage	30 weeks
Carrots	10 weeks	Cauliflower	20 weeks
Courgettes (zucchini)	10 weeks	Celery	28 weeks
Kohl rabi	10 weeks	Kale	28 weeks
Lettuce	8 weeks	Leeks	28 weeks
Peas	10 weeks	Maincrop onions	24 weeks
Early potatoes	10 weeks	Parsnips	28 weeks
Radishes	5 weeks	Maincrop potatoes	22 weeks
Turnips	8 weeks		

These figures are typical times for a cool temperate climate.

concentrate on these, sowing the same kind repeatedly throughout the season rather than growing slower maincrops.

Always use an early variety for late sowings in case of premature frost, and match plants to your needs: if you want to clear areas in one go, combine vegetables that mature simultaneously. Otherwise, balance sprinters and stayers to make the most of available space and gaps.

Permanent Crops

Perennial vegetables such as asparagus, globe artichokes, perennial broccoli and mercury (Good King Henry) need permanent homes, either in a separate bed or as feature plants. Asparagus (which need not be grown in special beds), seakale and artichokes are decorative enough to grow in flower beds. Mercury needs a position with light shade where it can be covered with straw to force early growth, while perennial broccoli is hardy enough to shelter early sowings or less robust vegetables.

Crop Groups

Legumes – the pea/bean family. Their roots manufacture nitrogen, helping both soil and neighbouring plants. They like deeply prepared, fertile ground. Dwarf kinds crop soonest, but taller varieties give heavier yields. Different bean varieties have red, white or mauve flowers, sometimes bi-coloured, followed by green, yellow, purple or speckled pods. Grow tall kinds in rows as windbreaks and divisions, or on tripods for extra stability and as formal features.
Brassicas – the cabbage family. These can follow legumes in rotation. As they like firm soil, simply cut down exhausted legumes, leaving their nutritious roots to decay, dress the soil with lime and plant brassicas. Curly kale, Savoy cabbages and red Brussels sprouts are the most ornamental, cauliflowers the hardest to grow well.
Rootcrops – Since these do not like fresh manure or lime, they can follow brassicas and need only a dressing of fertilizer to supplement residues from previous fertility. Most are biennial, so one or two plants can be left in to flower and provide seed for future seasons. Radish seedpods are a notable delicacy. Grow maincrops for winter storage, early varieties for immediate use.
Onions – These can be grown with legumes, or occupy a permanent plot year after year, providing plants remain healthy. This is a diverse family that includes leeks, chives, garlic and shallots as well as other alliums. Red or white-skinned onions look attactive. Maincrops can be demanding and untidy, although perennial and spring onions are neater and occupy less room. Tree onions are fascinating, clusters of new bulbs forming at the tips of tall flowering stems.

LEFT: *A small patch of thyme mats can be grown near the house.*

OPPOSITE: *Exquisitely organized formal herb garden with topiary. Herb gardens are ideal settings for topiary and ornamental features.*

but could be difficult to maintain. You might want to concentrate on medicinal herbs, dye plants or variegated cultivars. The choice is enormous but should be made at an early stage.

PLANNING THE HERB GARDEN

Sites and Structure

In its broadest, non-botanical sense, a herb is any plant with some part useful to man. This would include everything from greater celandine and mistletoe, both medicinal plants, to horsetail (equisetum) for cleaning brass, and sweet cicely, a natural sweetener. Only a relative handful of available herbs is normally grown in gardens, however, most of them for culinary use as flavourings and *bouquets garnis* (classic combinations of parsley, sage, thyme, savory, marjoram and sweet bay).

If these are the only herbs required, it is enough to allocate them a small accessible patch, about 4ft/1.2m × 6ft/1.8m and preferably sited near the kitchen. They are easy to grow, and frequent use will ensure they do not get out of hand. Herb collections tend to expand, though, and you may find yourself progressing from a small border to contemplating an elaborately designed herb garden. A little more experience of plant behaviour and requirements will then be necessary: whereas Mediterranean herbs, many of them silver or grey, thrive in full sun and Spartan conditions, green leafy plants such as parsley, mint and lovage prefer cool moist shade and annual herbs like rich kitchen garden soils.

It helps first to organize your ideas and decide whether you would like a classic formal herb garden, perhaps designed in an interesting geometrical pattern, or a relaxed cottage garden arrangement, which will certainly look charming

It is rarely possible to give every herb its perfect position. Fortunately most are more adaptable than commonly thought, providing you avoid heavy shade which will suppress flavours and alter leaf colouring. A sunless site is the least suitable, as is exposure to wind: some taller herbs are brittle and easily injured, while a still atmosphere encourages the pervasive fragrance usually associated with herb gardens.

When deciding where to grow any herb, try to visualize the plant's natural habitat. Wild thyme and rosemary, for example, colonize sun-baked rocky hillsides, while sweet woodruff nestles beneath trees and shrubs and horseradish can be rampant on damp banks. The majority of herbs resent water-logged conditions, though, and correcting drainage problems is more important than raising soil fertility.

A Framework

Because herbs vary so much in appearance and growth rate, and are often planted as single specimens, any collection can look aimless unless organized by a strong layout. Thoughtfully planned paths assist this definition, and also provide easy access for gathering and tending plants. Paths need not be as wide as those in kitchen gardens, nor as strictly functional: stepping stones set in chamomile, pennyroyal and other prostrate herbs will serve the purpose. Bricks or broken pavers are the most complementary materials, with small creeping herbs such as lemon thyme set in their joints.

Neat edges to beds reinforce the discipline imposed by the arrangement of pathways. As with herbaceous borders, tall herbs are placed at the back, or in the middle of island beds, while low-growing herbs should be near the front. Many of these can serve as edging plants: chives, parsley, thyme and marjoram are suitable, together with plants of less familiar herbal virtue such as alpine strawberries, thrift, sweet violets and pinks.

Restrained mat-forming herbs can be allowed to spill informally onto paths to soften their outline, or you might prefer to keep a cleanly defined margin, edging beds with a hard material such as tiles, a course of bricks, or low boards as used in medieval gardens. On heavy damp soils, deeper edging boards create raised beds with improved drainage.

ABOVE: *Small herb bed edged with trimmed ivy, a cheaper alternative to box and as neat.*

OPPOSITE: *Embroidered knot in box – such a pattern, although intricate, could be used to contain neat low-growing herbs.*

Herb Hedges

Beds in classic herb gardens, where every plant had a purpose, were enclosed by dwarf hedges kept strictly trimmed, which served the dual-purpose of enforcing formality and providing material for harvest. Any woody evergreen that tolerates clipping two to three times annually is ideal.

Choice of variety depends as much on scale as appearance – germander and box can be kept to 6in/15cm high for small beds and low plants, whereas some lavender and rosemary varieties will make dense hedges up to 3ft/90cm high around more ambitious borders. Try using hedging plants to provide contrast, planting a grey hedge, for example, to frame green herbs or those with brilliant flowers such as bergamot and evening primrose.

To make a good hedge quickly, most herbs must be spaced 6 – 9in/15 – 22cm apart, an easy and inexpensive project if grown from cuttings inserted at the right time through a strip of black polythene sheeting. Clip plants at an early stage to encourage dense growth.

Parterres

Much of the delight of a formal herb garden lies in its neat pattern of beds. Many such gardens are virtually perennial versions of summer carpet bedding, an approach that can be used even in small spaces.

Arrange a few herbs in a circle or square quartered by crossing paths, or in a semicircular bed with radiating spokes of helichrysum or clipped rue, and you have a miniature parterre, essentially any formal and balanced pattern of beds. They are usually planted with low-growing species to allow an uninterrupted overall view of their symmetry. Simplicity and neatness are more important than size. Keep to basic herb species and repeat their arrangement in each part of the design. Mulching the soil around the plants with gravel improves clarity and contrast.

Knot Gardens

A knot garden is a more intricate parterre, enclosed, divided and embroidered with dwarf hedges so that they weave in flowing patterns and interlace in knots. This kind of garden, excellent for organizing attractive herbs, needs frequent loving attention to maintain its sharply defined lines. Dwarf box is the classic hedging material, with silver, gold and dark green cultivars available to distinguish the separate threads making up knots.

Lonicera nitida grows faster but needs monthly clipping, whereas once or twice a year is enough for box once established. Dwarf forms of lavender, rosemary, thyme and germander are equally appropriate. Centres and corners can be embellished with simple topiary.

Herbs in Context

Increasing experience with the great diversity of herbs worth growing will introduce you to distinctive plants such as mugwort with its deeply divided silver-grey foliage, statuesque and yellow-flowered elecampane, or coarsely handsome comfrey whose flower racemes are rich purple and prolific. Place them dramatically to exploit their magnificence.

Many prostrate herbs make ideal ground cover around larger plants, and can even be used for paths where traffic is light. Wild thyme (*Thymus serpyllum*) and golden thyme (*T. vulgaris aureus*) are tough and durable, with the bonus of many attractive flowers that bees love in summer. Trailing forms of rosemary will carpet great areas and can be underplanted with dwarf bulbs. Fragrant sweet woodruff is excellent ground cover for impoverished soil such as that found beside privet hedges. Marjoram, creeping savory and golden sage all form extensive mats.

Stone sundials, statues and fountains are traditional features for marking the centre of radiating beds and supplying focal incident throughout the year, but tall evergreen herbs also serve this purpose. Sweet bay is an outstanding tree that tolerates pruning to maintain shape and size; cytisus (broom) and taller varieties of rosemary and lavender are equally striking.

Within beds highlights can be seasonal, using bold herbs such as angelica or sweet cicely, flowering shrubs or standard roses. Alternatively, urns and chimney pots make handsome features and ideal containers for trailing herbs and summer bedding plants.

As already suggested, numerous plants now usually regarded as flowers also have curative or culinary value, often the reason for their first being brought into cultivation. Primroses and cowslips, lily of the valley and heartsease (*Viola tricolor*) merit places in the herb garden where they add floral colour and fragrance.

Heathers too, medicinal plants popular with bees, share the same cultural needs as Mediterranean plants and make neat edgings for beds. In folklore the elderberry plays a

ABOVE: *The statuesque elecampane.*
OPPOSITE: *Standard rose 'The Fairy' above a carpet of borage.*

guardian role over herbs. With its graceful appearance, scented flowers and coloured berries, it is a particularly apt and attractive tree for the herb garden, especially in one of its variegated, cut-leafed or double-flowered forms.

Perennials supply continuity and therefore form the main component in any herb garden design. Some of the most popular herbs are annuals, however, and provision must be made for growing basil, borage, dill or coriander. Unless seedlings appear of their own accord from previous crops, seed must be sown afresh each spring.

It might prove simpler to grow these as kitchen garden plants in rows or patches: basil and parsley are fine edging plants for vegetable beds. Dill in any case should be kept well away from fennel, a common herb garden perennial with which it hybridizes to produce useless seedlings.

Alternatively, leave space around bushy perennials such as lemon balm, bergamot or winter savory, and sow the smaller annual herbs broadcast as companion plants. Borage, though, is a robust sprawling annual, popular with bees and therefore ideal for massing in drifts beneath fruit trees or shrub roses.

The thornless blackberry 'Oregon' with its decorative leaves twines around a post. Valerian adds colour.

A PLACE FOR FRUIT

Few gardens have room for a traditional orchard, and even one or two full-size apple trees will shade a large area of ground. A gooseberry or black currant bush takes as much room as a flowering shrub, often with a more limited season of appeal.

Fortunately there are space-saving ways to include all kinds of fruit in the kitchen garden, some of them decorative enough to merit a place as features in the herb garden. The widespread use of dwarfing rootstocks and a revival of artistic pruning to limit size ensure that most fruits can be incorporated into the garden without competing too much with other plants for light and nutrients.

Fruit for Small Gardens

As mentioned already, strawberries (including variegated and alpine kinds) have great potential as edgings for paths and borders, and as ground cover around larger shrubs. Although the tall flexible stems of raspberries need tying in place, a sunny fence can be used for this and for supporting blackberries and other bramble fruits. In confined spaces it is worth concentrating on the less vigorous thornless varieties, especially those with pretty foliage such as the fern-leafed *Rubus laciniatus*.

Always choose compact or upright varieties of currants and gooseberries, which you can prune to a manageable size or train into two-dimensional decorative forms. Apples and pears are best kept small by using the most dwarfing rootstocks, while cherries and plums (which can still grow large even on dwarfing rootstocks) need training on walls or thinning to allow plenty of light to filter through their spreading branches to plants below.

Aspects and Sites

The cultural needs of fruit vary: strawberries, cooking apples and rhubarb can tolerate shade, plums prefer deep moisture-retentive soils, while red currants and Morello cherries will flourish on cold sunless walls. Generally speaking, though, good light ripens the best fruit and well-drained ground helps avert pest and disease problems. Shelter from cold winds at blossom time ensures full crops, and most varieties benefit from moist soils or copious watering while their fruits are developing.

Walls and Fences

The boundary fences of a small enclosed garden can accommodate a large and varied amount of soft and top fruit trained as fans, cordons or espaliers, or cane berries tied to wires attached to the fence posts. The extra warmth of sunlit walls and fences often advances ripening, whereas fruit facing away from the sun matures later. You can

Fan-trained Morello cherry tree in flower; it will fruit well on a shady wall.

exploit these local variations in temperature to extend the harvesting season of a particular crop or to confer protection on tender fruits in cold gardens.

As varieties crop at different times, careful selection can spread maturity over a long period. Do not risk early flowering or late ripening kinds in cold districts in case of frost injury. Fruit is as prone to ailments as any other cultivated plant, so check when ordering that stocks have a relevant certificate of good health, and in particular that they are free from virus infections. Some varieties are more pest and disease resistant than others,

Apples and pears are the easiest to grow and to train in restricted forms such as bushes, cordons and espaliers, or even maintain for several years in pots. Distinguish between early varieties to be eaten immediately, and later ripening kinds that will store and which you may want to grow in greater quantity.

Plums, peaches and cherries need a little more care with pruning to keep growth within bounds without sacrificing yield. Like apples and pears, they are beautiful at blossom time, but their fruit, irresistible to birds, needs netting and will also need some lime in the soil to develop properly. In cool gardens the choicest varieties are best fan-trained on a sunny wall.

Many varieties of top fruit will not crop well or at all unless pollinated by another different variety; cherries and plums are notorious in this respect. Self-fertile varieties can be grown on their own, although even these crop more heavily if fertilized by another variety nearby. A good nursery catalogue will classify varieties into compatible groups to aid selection.

a valuable insurance where problems are known to exist.

Top Fruit

Fruits that would normally grow as trees if left unpruned are classified as top fruit. They include figs, mulberries, quinces and peaches, as well as the more familiar apples, pears, plums and cherries. Most are bought in a number of different forms or as young maidens (whips) for you to train yourself. The rootstock on which a chosen variety is grafted will affect a tree's ultimate size and yield: apples, pears, peaches, apricots, cherries and plums are available on dwarfing or semi-dwarfing rootstocks. Otherwise choose less vigorous varieties, especially those with restrained upright growth, to reduce the amount of corrective pruning needed.

Soft Fruit

'Soft fruit' is an arbitrary expression gardeners use to distinguish between tree-like top fruit and those which more closely resemble woody shrubs and climbers, or even herbaceous plants in the case of strawberries. Many kinds can be trained ornamentally, pruned to fit into confined spaces. They are good value in terms of yield and will crop for many years.

Bush Fruits

These naturally bushy plants (as distinct from top fruit grown in bush form) include gooseberries, and red, white and black currants. Although some, such as blueberries and hazelnuts (filberts), must normally be kept as shrubs, red and white currants are often grown flat on walls or fences where they are easily netted against birds. The less vulnerable gooseberries make excellent cordons and fans, tied to horizontal wires across the garden or flanking paths. Even black currants, conventionally grown as shrubs, will tolerate training on a fence. All kinds are self-fertile and need well-drained soil.

Cane Fruits

Raspberries crop in summer or autumn. Both kinds need annual renewal pruning: their fruited stems are cut at ground level and

replaced by new canes tied to wires. Compared with bush fruits they are therefore less adaptable as perennial features, although grown in rows they make novel living fences and divisions within the garden. Blackberries and hybrid berries need similar support for their long flexible canes, or you can grow the more decorative kinds on pillars, arches and tunnels.

Strawberries

As well as being grown for edging or in beds for three to four years before replacement, strawberries crop heavily if treated as a one-year crop. They then fit in rotation amongst the more heavily manured vegetables. Discard plants after fruiting and transplant runners to a new site.

Pruning and Training

In addition to satisfying their routine cultural requirements, it is important to remember that size and shape are also critical aspects of growing fruit in herb and kitchen gardens. As part of a coherent design their pleasing outlines need regular maintenance, as does their natural tendency to dominate neighbouring plants. Effective pruning aims to balance good crops and healthy growth with more cosmetic considerations.

Renewal pruning, used for raspberries and other cane fruits, is the simplest kind. Old fruited stems are removed, and new ones tied in their place. A similar principle applies to the sideshoots of peaches and some cherries, but here the basic framework of branches remains from one year to the next.

Spur pruning is a method of cutting off excess growth to retain a permanent system of fruiting spurs or stubby sideshoots. This is mainly used for apples and pears, although some apple varieties are tip-bearers and fruit at the ends of long sideshoots; the spur pruning approach would cut these off and ruin crops.

Training reinforces pruning to create and maintain a particular form of growth consistent with good cropping and appearance. Cane fruits are simply trained evenly onto wires and trelliswork, but plants with more rigid stems need a combination of techniques to restrain any wayward tendencies. Top fruit training is often only effective, though, if a rootstock of suitable vigour has been chosen.

Some kind of support is essential, at least initially, and this usually takes the form of vertical posts with horizontal wires, supplemented by diagonal canes for immature fans and oblique cordons. Stems are tied at the required angle while still young and soft, but after a few years the supports may often be removed. Festooning is a method of training weeping fruit trees, especially plums and pears, by bending their tall flexible stems into graceful arcs.

A step-over apple espalier grown on strong horizontal wire.

Pear cordons trained on diagonal wires save on space. An underplanting of daffodils turns a utilitarian feature into a decorative one.

Incidental Pleasures

Fruit trees and bushes are rewarding elements in the design of a garden. Most top fruits look attractive both in flower and in bearing, and when trained meticulously their orderly outlines echo and complement the ground plan of paths and beds. Fruit-growing can become compulsive, however, a possibility that might alter your garden plans.

Nineteenth-century French gardens sometimes resembled galleries of fruit displayed in an extravagant variety of designs such as palmettes, interwoven lattices and rounded arcures. You can transform a kitchen garden path into an ornate *allée* by flanking it with fruit trained in this way without sacrificing too much ground. Single cordon apples and pears need be spaced only 2ft/60cm apart, so allowing a number of different varieties to be grown in a fruiting sequence.

Varieties

Over the years gardens have been unique sanctuaries for old fruit cultivars disdained by market growers and so threatened with possible extinction. Many of these are at their best freshly picked and are therefore ideal for home cultivation. Allow room in your design for a few of these, as they are now becoming more widely available again. Many regions have old local varieties, probably more suitable for the soil and micro-climate of your garden than all-purpose commercial kinds.

Where good supplies of popular fruits are available locally, it may not be worth also giving them garden room. Instead, you could grow more elusive kinds such as purple or golden raspberries, Worcesterberries and the less common hybrid brambles – boysenberry, marionberry or King's Acre Berry, for example. Mulberries, quinces and red gooseberries often only occur as garden crops, while figs, greengages and, in mild areas, kumquats can be trained on warm house walls.

THE VERTICAL DIMENSION

A garden without height lacks vitality. It can be viewed at a glance, offers no enticement to explore, and in winter may appear desolate. Although the ground plan is a practical priority in designing herb and kitchen gardens, vertical interest should be considered at an early stage.

Incorporating tall plants and structures in the garden will transform its impact. Their cunning deployment can screen eyesores, enhance the importance of a path or focal point, add elements of mystery and surprise by hiding parts of the garden, and even appear to widen or lengthen its shape. Height must be consistent with the other dimensions of a bed or view, however. Standard apple trees, for example, might blend into a large kitchen garden, whereas a short standard gooseberry on a 2 – 3ft/60 – 90cm stem would be more appropriate in a bed of perennial herbs.

Since cold winds adversely affect the performance of most vegetables, fruits and herbs, the provision of shelter is a wise precaution when designing a garden. Height is directly related to the area protected, and a wall will shelter a distance up to ten times its size, although excessive shade can be a problem with very high structures.

There may be no choice, of course, with boundary walls, fences or hedges, where these are already in place. Purpose-built walls are expensive but, like fences, offer additional growing space for trained plants. Solid boundaries, however, cause wind turbulence within the garden, and it is often preferable to plant a tall hedge or shelter belt to filter strong winds and so reduce their impact. For more localized windbreaks to protect sensitive plants, consider decorative or fruiting hedges of roses, lavender or gooseberries, rows of raspberries, and tall vegetables such as Jerusalem artichokes and runner beans.

ABOVE AND OPPOSITE: *Height can be achieved with stick crops or by erecting decorative features.*

Pillars and Pergolas

Timber structures, traditionally known as 'carpentry', are aesthetically satisfying, although not as durable as those made from synthetic materials. Rustic woodwork suits the cottage garden style, while planed or 'finished' timber has a more formal air. Using pressure-treated wood or painting it with a suitable preservative will considerably extend the life of structures.

Single vertical poles, set deeply and securely in the ground, provide simple and instant accents in a view. They are often used to support climbing roses, tied in spirally to encourage flowering over the full height of the pillar. Groups of raspberries can be planted around the base and secured with loops of string, while a weeping grape vine, trained as a single stem to the top where its branches arch over a metal hoop, creates an inspired centre-piece for a bed. Three or four thinner poles, tied together at the top make stable tripods or pyramids for annual and perennial climbers.

Overhead Fruiting

A regular series of pillars joined by horizontal timbers forms a pergola, ideal for supporting more substantial plants. Grape vines and top fruits are particularly suitable for training to cover one of these. It was once customary in Japan to grow pears on pergolas so that the fruit hung within reach but was protected from predators by a canopy of foliage. Stout timbers are necessary for building pergolas, although more slender materials are adequate for tunnel structures over paths, especially if these are intended only to support marrows, runner beans, sweet peas and other annuals.

Disguise and Decoration

Carefully trained fruit and vegetables make effective screens to ensure seclusion or hide an unwanted view. A rosemary hedge, for example, can be planted to enclose an area for dustbins, wheelbarrows or a compost heap. Runner beans will reach 8ft/2.4m or more: grown on a straight row of bamboo canes, they develop into dense windbreaks for less robust plants or colourful screens to divide a kitchen garden into several 'rooms'. They can even be trained on tripods or teepees arranged in a circle around less decorative plants such as Brussels sprouts or plain-leafed rootcrops. As a more exotic screen around an intimate patio, weave an open fence of bamboo canes to support a combination of marrows, gourds and ipomoea (morning glory).

Left: *Bamboo arch used for runner beans, its stem disguised by maize.*

Opposite: *An arcade of pear trees frames a path.*

Crops for Height

Before buying top fruit, try to assess its eventual height when full grown. Some varieties are naturally taller than others, especially if their habit is predominantly upright. Rootstocks are one important influence – an apple on a very dwarfing stock may never exceed 6 – 8ft/1.8 – 2.4m, whereas the most vigorous stock will take it to 30ft/9m. Shape is another consideration. Although nursery practice varies, bush trees normally have 2ft/60cm stems, half-standards 4ft/1.2m, and full standards 6ft/1.8m high trunks. Form and ultimate height affect the spacing between trees, and this may be anything between 18 – 24in/45 – 60cm for cordons and 20ft/6m for standard pears and cherries.

Climbing fruit and vegetables that twine or cling with tendrils are especially valuable to the design-conscious gardener because of their versatility. Grape vines can be trained permanently in a number of styles, but even some annual crops grow quickly into dramatic vertical features.

The cucurbit family is noted for its large colourful flowers and bold foliage – trailing marrows and outdoor cucumbers will clothe a tunnel over a kitchen garden path, while the less territorial courgettes, normally grown on the flat, will adapt to short stakes for training as productive dwarf standards that economize on space.

Climbing peas and beans are ornamental subjects for screens, arches and trellis panels, either on their own or mixed with sweet peas for additional colour. They will even hitch an opportunist ride on tall crops such as artichokes and sweet corn, or scramble up evergreen hedges and windbreaks to relieve any uniformity with coloured flowers and pods.

Houseplants

Stepping from the house into the garden can sometimes seem an abrupt transition. House walls, though, are ideal sites for trained fruit, whose luxuriance will help soften the starkest building. A pear on a vigorous rootstock will clothe the wall of a two-storey house with blossom, foliage and fruit, and even add decorative relief in winter if its branches are trained precisely.

Vegetables, too, are useful in this respect. Climbing beans have a tropical flamboyance grown on a temporary porch of bamboo canes, which could echo a similar arangement on an archway further from the house. Shed and garage walls are other potential sites for fruit and vegetables, either perennials trained on permanent wires, or annuals on vertical netting or strings secured to eaves.

Crown imperials (Fritillaria imperialis) beneath an espaliered apple tree.

FLOWERS FOR PRODUCTIVE GARDENS

Only purists would object to the inclusion of flowering plants in herb and kitchen gardens. They have as much right to be there as poppies in cornfields, and almost as long a history: in the early seventeenth century William Lawson recommended numerous flowers for the 'Country Housewife's Garden', primarily a place for edible plants. His suggestions, which included irises, hollyhocks and pot marigolds, are still valid, although there are countless other species worth introduction. They could be surplus to flower garden requirements or planted purposely for cutting – sweet Williams, gladioli and hardy annuals, for example. Pathside borders make ideal nursery beds for perennials raised from seed and awaiting transplanting.

Bulbs

Flowering bulbs look well planted at the base of fruit trees, while dwarf early-flowering kinds such as snowdrops and *Crocus tommasinianus* cultivars brighten up deciduous fruit bushes before the latter come into leaf. All the allium species (onion family) are particularly appropriate, as are crown imperials (*Fritillaria imperialis*) which spread into stately groups at strategic points. St Brigid and de Caen anemones relish rich kitchen garden conditions. Most suitable of all are saffron crocuses (*C. sativus*), a traditional condiment that is expensive to buy.

Classic Climbers

Kitchen garden paths were traditionally lined with flowering climbers as alternatives to hedges or trained fruit. Clematis and honeysuckle give colour and fragrance both here and on arches or arbours in herb gardens. Old-fashioned roses add a sense of timelessness and thrive in well-manured surroundings. Ramblers such as 'Phyllis Bide', 'Francis E. Lester' and 'Veilchenblau' will climb into large fruit trees, or can be trained on pillars joined by loosely-slung ropes; growing them in this way together with hops is a classic Edwardian conceit.

Flower Crops

Eating the bright yellow blooms as well as the fruits of courgettes is fashionable, but using other flowers for flavouring and garnishes is almost a forgotten custom. Exploring the range of plants once grown for these purposes can increase the diversity of colourful flowers with a legitimate place in the herb and kitchen gardens.

Flower petal salad; this mixture can be grown entirely from seed supplied in a single packet by the seedsman.

Borage is a robust annual herb best grown in the kitchen garden where it will often seed itself freely. Seedlings are readily transplanted, but allow each plenty of room to sprawl or be prepared to support plants. The brilliant blue flowers can be floated in drinks, or added to summer salads with those of nasturtiums, another annual that will either climb vigorously or make pretty ground cover according to variety. Pot marigolds (calendula), sweet violets, pansies and peonies have all been used to decorate dishes, and grow well amongst their productive neighbours.

Many herbs are renowned for their attractive flowers, some of which also have culinary value, so leave room for extra plants if you plan to crop them frequently. Laven-der flowers, usually gathered for *pot pourri* and pomanders, were traditionally used too for flavouring vinegar, as were the flowers of rosemary, hyssop and tarragon. The more fragrant pinks earn their place amongst herb border edgings with their former use as clove flavouring. Rose and broom buds made popular pickles, their flowers also being used in quantity to make country wines.

Flowering chives make an ornamental companion for the double-flowered lychnis.

Flowering Vegetables

Where pods and other fruits are the main purpose of cultivation, plants must of course be left to flower. Many, such as those of marrows, broad beans and climbing peas, are particularly outstanding. Leaf and root crops, though, often only flower after 'bolting', when they are generally pulled up as useless. They still have decorative value, nevertheless, enhancing the kitchen garden with their novelty and providing self-reliant gardeners with home-grown seeds. Use them judiciously, for some set copious quantities of seed that may become a nuisance.

The most spectacular plants in flower are rhubarb, lovage, angelica and parsnips, all of which can reach 8ft/2.4m high. The perennials are best cut down before actually seeding, but a single parsnip plant will yield several ounces of seed that often germinate more readily than bought supplies.

Chicory flowers are large and clear blue, a scarce colour that always attracts attention. Salsify has exotic purple daisies, while those of the perennial scorzonera are brilliant yellow; the flowers of both are edible. Seakale produces enormous inflorescences – the individual creamy flowers are insignificant, but a complete head is a magnificent sight,

The wide flat heads of Sedum spectabile *attract both butterflies and bees.*

and if left to set seed will change into a broad cluster of white capsules that can be dried for indoor decoration.

It is sometimes said that allowing herbs to bloom dilutes the flavour of their foliage, but any change is minor compared with the beauty of their flowers. Chives make an ornamental edging at all times, but most of all when covered with their mauve drumstick flowers. Carpeting herbs such as thyme, marjoram and pennyroyal flower inexhaustibly for weeks on end without noticeable harm. Sweet woodruff, the ultimate ground cover herb, is studded in early summer with dainty white stars, at which stage it is perfect for cutting and drying.

Wildlife Plants

Whereas commercial growers often prefer to raise their crops in relatively sterile surroundings where any insect is suspect as a pest, gardeners tend to be more tolerant, especially as many insects are beneficial or simply pleasant to have around. However, it is worth learning to distinguish harmless moths and butterflies, for example, from those whose larvae can injure fruit and vegetable crops, for some such as codling moth, gooseberry sawfly and large white butterflies are major crop pests.

Although purely decorative, butterflies bring colour and life to the garden as they forage amongst open flowers for nectar. The larvae of natural pest predators such as hoverflies, lacewings and parasitic wasps have voracious appetites, each of them consuming dozens of aphids daily. Encourage them by growing flowers with large flat heads – asters, achillea and sedum are typical plants these valuable short-lived allies find easy to graze.

ABOVE: *Dark-leafed red mountain spinach or orach.*

OPPOSITE: *The globular heads of the rose 'Raubritter' peer through a veil of bronze fennel.*

ENCOURAGING DIVERSITY

Tendencies towards smaller gardens can present a serious obstacle to segregated herb and kitchen garden cultivation. There may not be room for dedicating a worthwhile patch to the plants, or doing so might leave an unacceptably reduced area for flower beds.

In such cases you can avoid drastic upheaval by integrating vegetables, fruit and herbs into established flower beds, an imaginative compromise that blends economy with flair. If flowering plants look right in a kitchen garden context, it is reasonable to expect vegetables in their turn to merge happily into flower borders, especially where these are designed in a relaxed rather than formal way.

Some crops insinuate themselves into other areas: salsify, asparagus, parsley, fennel and even tomatoes seed themselves given a chance, sometimes making successful combinations with flowers. Other cropping plants need to be introduced cautiously, though.

Cutting a cabbage leaves a conspicuous gap, whereas pulling a few carrots or picking runner beans will not destroy an arrangement.

Deciding where to grow utility plants largely depends, therefore, on their habit. According to type, they can be grouped in small blocks or along edges, dispersed as trained features or startling highlights, or strategically used as specimen foliage plants and formal bedding. 'Permaculture' describes the logical conclusion to this, with perennial flowers and crops allowed to blend freely in a varied and harmonious permanent cottage garden arrangement.

Tall Vegetables in Herbaceous Borders

The back of a border is the best place for tall imposing plants, some of them so good-looking that they are worth growing even if you dislike them as vegetables. Globe artichokes and cardoons are magnificent grey-leafed thistles that need manure to sustain their 5–6ft/1.5–1.8m stature. Some varieties of Jerusalem artichoke, which can reach 6–8ft/1.8–2.4m tall, have attractive large yellow daisy flowers. Sweet corn planted in small blocks resembles a group of larger grasses or bamboo, while cane wigwams covered with climbing beans (grown in Britain only as an ornamental until last century) make luxuriant and colourful vegetable topiary.

Mid-border Plants

Asparagus, salsify and scorzonera belong here, and are effective when combined with kniphofia, gypsophila or day lilies. Some rhubarb varieties have brilliant red stems as well as outrageous weed-smothering leaves. For extra foliar colour, a mixture of Swiss chard varieties will produce plants with gold, red or white stems. Slender red mountain spinach (orach) is best sown *en masse*: pinch the tips for a bushy effect. Curly or red-leafed brassicas are excellent foliage plants, remaining in winter to complement spring bedding and evergreen shrubs.

The rose 'Lavender Pinocchio' with blue rue.

Feverfew with Geranium psilostemon.

Dwarf Plants

Lettuce, carrots, beetroot and red-leafed chicories are adaptable edging plants, or can be grown in small groups near the front of a border. Here uniformity may be desirable, and it is worth choosing F1 hybrid varieties to ensure consistent height and appearance. Use fast-growing or forcing types to harvest before their foliage loses its freshness, and re-sow or transplant immediately to fill spaces with successional interest.

Dispersing Herbs and Fruit

As in designated herb and kitchen gardens, fruit trees and bushes have an indispensable structural role in addition to their obvious decorative qualities. Es-pecially in trained forms, they contribute permanence and a subtle stability to the natural exuberance of flower borders. Half-standard apples and pears are valuable for their height, and if sculpted as symmetrical goblets or pyramids resemble live statuary, whereas a festooned plum or cherry adds a whimsical touch to more formal borders.

Among smaller flowers, try growing standard red currants and gooseberries. Blueberries, which do not train successfully, are perfect companions for pieris and rhododendrons in an acid border. For a classic low fence to divide herbaceous plants from a path, train apples on dwarf rootstocks along 12–15in/30–37cm high wires as single horizontal espaliers, sometimes known as 'step-over' trees or cordons (see page 34).

Taller perennial herbs are natural shrubs, many of them evergreen with outstandingly attractive foliage. Forms of artemisia (wormwood, mug-wort or southernwood), lavender and rosemary can enhance the prominence of more flamboyant plants with their soft silvers and greys. Bold leafy herbs such as angelica and lovage need back-seat positions where they make an impressive impact with thalictrum, verbascum and other herbaceous giants.

At the other extreme savory, wild basil (calamintha), feverfew or sage mingle pleasantly on the edge of borders with pinks, herbaceous potentillas and nepeta (catmint). Some traditional herbs are more commonly regarded as flowering plants today: bergamot (monarda), tansy, foxgloves and eryngium (sea holly) blend well wherever grown, and are the best kinds to introduce first into a conventional herbaceous border.

Using brightly coloured vegetables to create carpet bedding is a purely ornamental tradition, since harvesting any plants will obviously ruin the display. However, the practice is easily extended in a less rigorous way to the kitchen garden, where you can satisfy decorative instincts by artistically grouping plants used leaf by leaf rather than gathered in their entirety.

The bedding vegetable familiar to most gardeners is ornamental or flowering cabbage. While young they are as palatable as edible kinds, and plants are quite mature before they develop their characteristic central rosettes in shades of yellow, white, pink and purple. Plant in bold groups for autumn and winter colour. Dwarf curly kale, once widely used for winter and spring bedding, is best raised in a nursery bed so that you can select uniform specimens for transplanting.

Flowering blocks of summer carpet bedding – ageratum, *Begonia semperflorens*, impatiens, for example – can be divided by lines of red cut-and-come-again lettuces, parsley and corn salad, with coloured chicory, red and gold beetroot, Swiss chard or perpetual spinach for central dot plants.

From using prostrate herbs

Red and green forms of lettuce, Begonia semperflorens *and lavender.*

in paths to planting them *en masse* as fragrant lawns is a short but logical step. Roman chamomile (*Anthemis nobilis* – not the annual German chamomile, *Matricaria recutita*) is the most familiar lawn herb, non-flowering cultivars quickly spreading to create an even sward with a

pleasant scent of apples when trodden upon. It is not very durable, however, and difficult to keep weed-free. Less demanding alternatives are the various low-growing thymes, pennyroyal, Coriscan mint (*Mentha requienii*) and heather, a noted medicinal and bee plant.

Spires of foxgloves behind nepeta and potatoes.

Wild Plants for Cultivation

The distinction between wild and cultivated flowers is as tenuous as that dividing flowers from herbs and vegetables, and also challenges the definition of a 'weed'. It does not take much lateral thought to appreciate that many weeds and wild flowers are both pretty and widely used as culinary, herbal or fruiting plants, and therefore might justify a place within the herb or kitchen garden. You should of course discriminate against rampant species likely to be invasive in good soils. Use wild plants medicinally only with great care.

Wild Fruits

There are many forms of elderberry (sambucus species and cultivars) worth growing for their flowers, fruits, which may be white as well as purple, and refined foliage – gold, variegated or lacily cut according to cultivar. Prune annually to maintain size and encourage young growth. Bilberries, huckleberries and ornamental hawthorns are all attractive plants with useful crops.

Wild Herbs

Apart from foxgloves and primroses, already popular as garden plants, there are numerous other wild flowers with medicinal or culinary uses. Good King Henry (mercury), for example, has nutritious leaves like spinach in use and appearance, but immature shoots can also be forced under pots in early spring. The annual scarlet pimpernel, perennial in warm gardens, is a bushy low-growing gem used for skin complaints, while soapwort or bouncing Bet (saponaria) has pink fragrant flowers and a reputation as a soap substitute. Greater celandine with its golden leaves and flowers is a traditional cure for warts; grow it beside scarlet poppies, blue delphiniums and broad beans with true cottage garden egalitarianism.

A tiny diversely planted bed with beetroot, chard, parsnips and carrots; nasturtium provide colour and flower petals.

Further Economies on Space

*E*ncouraging diversity and integration paradoxically saves space while growing more plants. This is achieved partly by eliminating some of the bare ground or pathways that must be left between rows and plants grown conventionally. Growing plants in several tiers or training them vertically, especially flat against walls and fences, also economizes on the amount of ground needed.

There are other savings to be made where space is at a premium. If you grow vegetables in straight rows, consider sowing two compatible kinds together. Parsnips, for example, can be sown at stations 9in/22.5cm apart with radishes to fill the intervening gaps; the latter germinate fast, marking the rows of slower growing parsnips, and will be cleared before the winter crop needs the room. Other slow, widely-spaced crops such as leeks, winter brassicas and salsify can be combined with fast varieties of carrots, lettuce or spring onions.

Radishes and lettuces are often sold in mixtures, the various types included usually maturing at different rates. By using these, several successional sowings can be combined in a single row that will crop over a long period. Dwarf, intermediate and tall peas sown together will, of course, need full-size supports but again will crop for a long time, while mixtures of bean seeds provide motley colour when plants flower and bear their pods.

The idea of blending vegetables has been taken a step further with the introduction of salad mixtures that can include a dozen or more plant types to cut over a whole year. Sow broadcast in patches or parallel rows a few inches apart, and pick individual leaves or trim strips with scissors.

ABOVE: *Wooden hanging container of courgettes and nasturtium.*

OPPOSITE: *Strawberry tower producing fruit from its pouches.*

THE POTTED GARDEN

Just as shortage of space is no obstacle to growing crop plants, so a total lack of available ground can be overcome by using pots, boxes and similar containers. Even an established garden often has paths, terraces and other areas of hardstanding that will look less barren if used to accommodate groups of urns or tubs.

The range of useful containers is infinite, from terracotta pots, strawberry towers and hanging baskets to used paint tins or a moist sink for growing watercress. For large-scale plantings, a raised bed is ideal and can be built with an existing hard surface as a foundation, using bricks, building blocks, boards or railway sleepers for the sides.

Clay and wooden pots last longer than plastic containers and usually blend more instantly into their surroundings, but plastic pots do not dry out so quickly and are therefore useful for crops that love moisture or where frequent watering is difficult to arrange. In very formal situations decorative urns, glazed pots or painted boxes may be more suitable, especially for fruit trees; traditional square Versailles pots are available with matching pyramid supports for climbing plants such as beans and gourds, or a cut-leafed blackberry.

Summer salads, compact vegetables and herbs can be grown in windowboxes, providing these are deep enough. Six inches (fifteen centimetres) is the minimum depth for any container to ensure unchecked growth without unreasonably frequent watering and feeding. A full box is heavy and so must be securely supported. Alternatively, face a window opening with a deep board and arrange pots behind on the sill. Some bush and trailing crops – miniature tomatoes, New Zealand spinach or bush basil, for example – do well in deep hanging baskets.

The smaller a container, the more dedicated your care must be, especially in hot or frosty weather: remember plants rely on you entirely for their welfare. Successful management depends on a number of factors, starting with drainage. At the bottom of any container (other than a hanging basket) you should spread a layer of hard, free-draining material such as stones, broken bricks or cinders. Make sure there are drainage holes, and raise pots off the ground with pieces of tile or slate.

Always use a good compost, preferably a heavy soil-based one for stability, and renew some of this each year where perennials are grown. Water regularly to maintain consistently moist soil, and feed at set intervals from about six weeks after planting, especially once pods or fruits start swelling. Protect containers from frost: if their contents freeze solid, plants can die from dehydration.

Variegated pineapple mint, spearmint and chives. The pretty Angel pelargoniums add extra colour.

Plant Combinations

Containers do not have to be devoted to a single specimen or crop. Even a small pot of dwarf French beans can have trailing lobelia or blue phacelia sown around the edge to make it look less functional. Larger containers and tubs may be planted as small gardens, to stand in important positions on a terrace or beside a doorway.

Around a tall central plant such as a mophead bay or a dwarf apple, you can combine a crop of compact lettuces with trailing petunias, or plant yellow courgettes to hang down the sides. A kitchen windowbox is a convenient place for mixing one or two parsley, basil or marjoram plants with more conventional summer bedding flowers.

Some Plants for Pots – Fruit

If suitable varieties are chosen and kept well watered and fed, there are few utility plants that will not thrive in containers. Fruit trees are particularly suitable for pots 12in/30cm or more in diameter, and can be most impressive if skilfully trained. Top fruits must be grafted on very dwarfing stocks unless you are highly expert at pruning. Fig trees, whose roots are notoriously unrestrained, crop more prolifically if confined to containers. Strawberries will fruit in pots both indoors and out, and perpetual (ever-bearing) varieties can be grown in towers or stacking pots as they also crop on their trailing runners.

Herbs

Strawberry towers are excellent for herb collections, especially compact forms of a single genus, such as the various cultivars of thyme or marjoram. A few herbs are invasive in open ground, and a large pot provides ideal restriction for mint, tarragon or horse radish. Dense evergreen herbs like rosemary, hyssop and germander can be clipped into simple topiary, and a few pots of these make a unique collection on a terrace or patio.

Vegetables

Peppers, cucumbers, tomatoes and other summer crops fruit well in 9 – 12in/22.5 – 30cm pots if you can keep them moist at all times, or they may be planted in wooden troughs or growing bags beside a wall where climbing varieties can be supported on strings. Plant spring-flowering bulbs in larger tubs, and then in summer grow runner beans on cane tripods to hide the dying bulb foliage. Loose-leaf lettuce and mixed salad seeds broadcast in a window box or container near the door will provide frequent summer pickings.

The Advantages of Glass

Glass cloches and handlights extend the growing season outdoors by protecting vegetable sowings and favourite herbs from frost. The range of plants you can grow, especially out of season, will be further expanded if you have a greenhouse. On large estates these were once an essential accessory in kitchen gardens, where they were often built as highly ornate lean-to structures against a garden wall. Some modern kinds are very attractive, and a circular or hexagonal model would make an intriguing centre-piece for a kitchen garden.

With little or no heat, in most districts supplies of herbs and salads can be maintained through the winter, with melons, cucumbers, tomatoes and other tender crops taking over in summer and autumn. Fruit may be planted in greenhouse borders for training up the sides, but a greenhouse is also very useful for over-wintering or forcing crops in pots. Strawberries will fruit up to two months earlier under glass, the blossom of choice pear, nectarine and

A dwarf lemon tree grows and fruits under glass, but benefits from being taken outdoors for the summer.

gage varieties in pots will be protected, while sensitive perennial herbs such as lemon verbena and Mexican sage (*Salvia azurea* 'Grandiflora') can survive in cold climates.

A cold frame functions like a miniature unheated greenhouse and is an equally valuable aid to herb and kitchen garden routines, both for raising new plants and for housing tender ones over winter. It is perhaps the ultimate container, where you can grow out-of-season vegetables and herbs, fruits such as melons and cucumbers in a cold summer, and crops that need blanching or forcing – rhubarb, seakale and self-blanching celery, for example.

Seakale is blanched by being covered in this ornamental pot.

THE FOUR SEASONS

Winter

This can be the quietest season, a good opportunity to tidy and plan beds and borders, clean up existing ones and even create the layout of new gardens. Paths and other constructions are best left until spring or autumn, though, when frost and rain are less likely to interrupt work. Providing the soil is not frozen, fruit trees and bushes can be planted; in severe frost move manure and compost onto vegetable beds while the ground is hard. On warm sunny days enjoy pruning top fruit to shape.

Vegetables In mild districts crops such as round-seeded peas and broad beans can be sown if the soil is friable. Under glass make early sowings, especially salads to grow in a cold frame. Try the nineteenth-century French custom of multiple sowings in frames: broadcast and rake in seeds of forcing carrots and turnips mixed, and then plant hardy lettuce or cauliflowers in the same soil. Force rhubarb and seakale by covering with pots.

Fruit Prune secondary growth on top fruit, or wait until flower buds are visible if you are uncertain. Old congested trees can have complete branches removed to admit light and improve their shape. Cover bush fruits where birds are likely to attack the buds. Start forcing strawberries in pots. Towards the end of winter watch out for welcome flowers and catkins on hazelnuts, and also the blooms of *Iris unguicularis*, best planted around plum and cherry trees to share their annual dressing of lime.

Herbs Knock snow from evergreen hedges and bushy herbs, and protect sweet bay in severe weather. Mint, chives and tarragon can all be potted up for forcing into growth. Early crocuses, winter aconites and snowdrops make a brilliant contrast with the greens and greys of perennial herbs.

Flowering alpine strawberries grow in shade under the mahogany-barked Prunus serrula.

Spring

This is a very busy season in the kitchen garden. Light soils can be dug, heavier ones reduced to a workable tilth for early sowings. Plan well ahead for succession and also prepare to sow winter vegetables. Spare time, though, to enjoy the exuberant displays of blossom and young growth while the year is still green and fresh.

Vegetables Sow little and often as the soil warms up, and in a dry season be prepared to mulch to maintain the vitality of young crops. Do not risk tender plants outdoors until frosts are past – find the average date of last frosts for your area and count back to calculate the best time to sow: six weeks is the average period between sowing and planting out.

Fragrant broad beans will be flowering now – grow dwarf kinds as edging or intercrop with coloured lettuce and oriental leaves.

Fruit Most kinds like feeding with manure or fertilizer as growth accelerates. Grapes, peaches and apricots may need disbudding to control vigour. You can now safely prune plums and cherries, whose wounds heal faster in spring and summer. As strawberries start to flower, tuck straw around them to conserve moisture and keep trusses clean.

Herbs New herbs can be planted and annual kinds sown: coriander, dill, purslane, borage and basil (in warmth). Early flowering herbs such as rosemary are clipped to shape as soon as blooms fade. Hard prune dwarf hedges early and start routine clipping towards the end of the season.

Summer

This is the season when you begin to reap the rewards of earlier labours. Congestion is a risk, with a number of crops maturing together, and may suggest the need to replan designs and sowing routines. Some plants demand regular watering and supplementary feedings to sustain growth. Everywhere should be bright with promise and colour, especially where flowers blend with utility crops.

Vegetables Clear crops as they finish and before growth becomes untidy or harbours pests and diseases. Successional sow for replacement, using early varieties towards the end of the season. Winter vegetables need planting out, and crops such as onions will be ripening. Decide whether to leave any plants to flower or set seed. There is still time to sow annuals such as scarlet flax, annual chrysanthemums and nigella for late colour or cutting.

Fruit Much of the interest will come from ripening fruit, especially on trained trees where summer pruning of excess growth will suddenly expose fruits to sunlight. Gather as soon as mature, and be prepared to thin heavy crops and net if necessary against predators. Strawberry beds can be cleared and the ground

ABOVE: *Clematis twines around fruiting espalier-grown pears.*

LEFT: *High summer in the integrated garden where phlox blossom beside parsnips.*

Autumn

Many crops now need gathering in before the frosts. Sunny days and cool nights induce leaves to start colouring with their autumn tints, and the productive garden can be a satisfying place if you also keep on top of tidying spent growth or late weeds. Give next year a thought, though, for seeds and new plants are best ordered now.

Vegetables In mild gardens many crops can be autumn sown, for winter supplies or to crop earlier next year, but where winters are very cold, sowings may not be worth the risk and it is better to push on with clearing and digging heavy soils. Remember to use cloches to protect late ripening crops and to cover sowings intended to winter outdoors.

Fruit Late fruits usually keep best, and should therefore be picked and stored with care. Peaches and cherries can be renewal pruned, with new shoots tied in securely before winter. Exhausted cane and bramble fruit stems are cut out entirely, the plants tucked up with a mulch of compost or manure to protect their crowns. From mid-autumn onwards you can start planting new fruit.

Herbs Most herbs will start to hibernate, some such as lovage and sweet cicely disappearing altogether until next spring. Protect those that remain – salad burnet, winter savory and sage, for example, are all safer under a thick mulch of autumn leaves in very cold gardens. A limited number of herbs can be potted to overwinter indoors, but from now onwards you will probably depend on supplies dried earlier.

prepared for new ones. Rhubarb may flower splendidly, but do not let it seed.

Herbs The majority of herbs flower this season, with extensive carpets of thyme, hyssop and marjoram attracting a host of bees and butterflies. Trim after flowering, and start deliberately harvesting herb shoots for drying late in the season. Take cuttings of any perennials you want to multiply or replace.

Figs prefer a light sandy soil. Good drainage helps prevent the production of too much leaf to fruit.

A BRIEF GUIDE TO GOOD HUSBANDRY

Soil Care

No soil is beyond redemption, but how to improve its condition so that a wide range of often demanding crops can be grown depends on first identifying its type. Simple observation can reveal whether it stays wet for a long time, which may indicate impaired drainage or heavy ground with a high clay content; rapid drying to a powdery consistency is a sign of light, sometimes impoverished soil.

Confirm your diagnosis by taking a handful of moist earth and rolling it into a ball. Light sandy soils will fall apart almost immediately. If the ball feels gritty but stays intact, it is a sandy loam with a higher clay content than the lightest soils. If you can polish the ball with your thumb to a shiny finish, it will probably contain about 50% clay (a medium loam), whereas pure clay is sticky and can be moulded into other shapes.

Light soils drain fast, warm quickly in spring and are easy to work. They are often infertile and dusty when dry. Clay on the other hand is potentially very fertile, but remains cold and wet for a long time in spring and is heavy to cultivate; when dry it sets like concrete. Medium loams combine the virtues of both extremes without their obvious disadvantages.

While good cultivation will adapt most soils to specific crop needs, in difficult cases it may be easier to match plants to the existing soil. Figs, raspberries, nuts, red currants, root crops and evergreen herbs prefer sandy light soil. Annual and leafy perennial herbs, on the other hand, together with plums, apples, brambles, black currants and the whole brassica family thrive on heavy ground. A medium loam suits most crops.

Fertility

It is important to distinguish between soil texture and fertility. An 'open' soil that is relatively pleasant to cultivate and able to sustain healthy plant growth has good texture. Decayed organic material (humus) is a key ingredient, stabilizing light soils and aerating clay. Garden compost, leafmould and other organic waste supply humus without significantly raising fertility. Many herbs demand little more than this.

Farmyard manure contains varying amounts of nutrients and therefore will improve fertility as well as texture. It is normally worked into kitchen garden soil every three to four years to support heavy-feeding plants – brassicas, potatoes and straw-berries – and can be spread annually around the greediest fruit: black currants, black-berries, rhubarb, for example. It is not essential, and may indeed be harmful, for the majority of herbs.

Fertility can also be raised by fertilizers. These, however, do nothing for soil texture and their use should be combined with some source of humus. Even where manure is used, fertilizers are valuable for stimulating quick growth early in the season – as a tonic for spring cabbages or flowering fruit, for example – or to feed late sowings in previously manured ground.

Water

No matter how lavishly fed, plants cannot absorb nutrients without water. Ideally you should aim for consistently moist soil during growth. Mulching, hoeing, close spacing and planting new stock in spring or autumn when soils are moist all help to avoid water-loss and plant stress. In times of drought concentrate water on seedlings, leaf crops, plants in flower or bearing, and any recently planted.

Sowing

Basic methods of sowing and planting are familiar to most gardeners, but following a few additional guidelines will help ensure success.

Always wait until the soil is warm enough before sowing, otherwise seeds can rot or germinate erratically.

Rhubarb has a greedy appetite for farmyard manure.

Above: *A mono-planting of leeks in late winter.*

Right: *Strawberries are netted against birds and strawed to prevent the fruit deteriorating from contact with muddy earth.*

In cold areas warm the soil first by covering it with cloches or clear plastic sheeting for two to three weeks. Keep the ground moist throughout germination, which can take up to eight weeks for parsley, parsnips and other slow crops.

In dry seasons flood the seed drills before sowing, and then fill with moist spent seed- or potting-compost. For small sowings amongst other plants, scribe parallel drills across the area, or press an inverted pot into the ground and sow a circle of seeds with the label in the centre. Always sow sparsely to avoid later thinning, although broadcast sowings are easily thinned by dragging a rake across the seedlings.

Planting

Plants enjoy their comfort, so be sure to water before and after planting, try not to disturb the roots when moving them, and never transfer plants straight from warmth into cold soil.

Container-grown specimens can be planted out any time the soil is tillable, although late spring and summer introductions will need regular watering until self-sufficient. Bare-rooted deciduous plants are best moved after leaf-fall, evergreens in mid-autumn or mid-spring. Provide adequate support for fruit trees before rather than after planting to prevent root damage.

Routine Aftercare

Small plants settle in quickly compared with larger trees and shrubs, which may need careful watering for a year or two afterwards, and support for even longer. Keeping new plants clear of weeds and other rivals aids rapid establishment. The stems of fruit trees can be surrounded with squares of carpet or black plastic sheeting to suppress weeds, while on dry soils or those difficult to weed, planting through black sheeting saves considerable labour. Herbs in particular will benefit: the plastic can be disguised with a layer of gravel and will prevent tenacious weeds from infiltrating the herbs.

Try to practise a few cultural refinements for really healthy plants. If you learn to spot poor colour and other signs of unthriftiness, you can rogue out or treat an ailing plant before a disorder becomes serious and possibly infectious. Thin and space plants so that each has enough room for all-round development, remove un-wanted shoots before they are too large, and pinch out stems and sideshoots to promote bushy growth.

Insure yourself against losses. Sometimes dormant plants will survive a hard winter, only to succumb to a late frost. If in doubt, protect plants with windbreak screens, frost insulation such as coverings of leaves or synthetic materials, and mulch to prevent injury during drought. Keep a few reserve plants in frames or seedbeds to substitute for casualties, and always take cuttings or save seed in case you lose the parent plant. Many perennials are short-lived, and anyway if you grow good plants other people will covet them, so a little extra propagation is never wasted.

LIST OF SUPPLIERS

The plants mentioned in this book are particular to the United Kingdom. Some of them may not be readily available in Australia. To seek out these plants or substitutes suitable to Australian conditions the following specialist and mail order nurseries could be consulted.

LEGEND (N) = Nursery (MO) = Mail Order (C) = Catalogue available.

New South Wales

Colonial Cottage Nursery
62 Kenthurst Road
Dural NSW 2158
(02) 654 1340
(N)

Engall's Nursery
155 Carlingford Road
Epping NSW 2121
(02) 876 2177
(N)

Ferguson's Garden Centre
408 Windsor Road
Baulkham Hills NSW
   2153
(02) 639 4044
(N)

The Fragrant Garden
25 Portsmouth Road
Erina NSW 2250
(043) 67 7322
(N) (C) (MO)

Greenjade Nursery
Silverdale Road
Wallacia NSW 2745
(047) 74 1112
(N) (C)

Hargraves Nurseryland
630 Old Northern Road
Dural NSW 2158
(02) 651 1833
(N)

Johnny Appleseed
   Nursery
cnr Richmond Road and
   Stone Street
Plumpton NSW 2761
(02) 625 8236
(N) (C)

Viburnum Gardens
8 Sunnyridge Road
Arcadia NSW 2159
(02) 653 2259
(N)

Queensland

Home Gardener's Centre
2765 Beaudesert Road
Calamvale QLD 4116
(07) 273 3966
(N) (C)

South Australia

McLaren Vale Garden
   Centre
174 Main Road
McLaren Vale SA 5171
(08) 323 8440
(N)

Victoria

Colonial Nurseries Pty Ltd
Emerald Road
Beaconsfield VIC 3807
(03) 707 3973
(N)

The Cottage Gardens
   Nursery
91 Doncaster Road
Baldwyn North VIC 3104
(03) 859 9330
(N) (C) (MO)

Hills-End Herb and
   Cottage Garden Plants
130 Homestead Road
Berwick VIC 3806
(03) 707 1143
(N) (MO)

Honeysuckle Farm
Mountain Highway
Sassafras VIC 3787
(03) 755 1508
(C)

Lilydale Herb Farm
61 Mangans Road
Lilydale VIC 3140
(03) 735 0486
(N) MO)

Linton's Nurseries
cnr Nepean Highway and
   Canadian Bay Road
Mt Eliza VIC 3930
(03) 787 2122
(N)

Mount Evelyn Garden
   Centre
26a York Road
Lilydale VIC 3140
(03) 736 1294
(N)

Poyton's Nursery
cnr Boulevard and Vida
   Streets
Essendon VIC 3040
(03) 337 8111
(N)

INDEX

A. M. Clevely studied English literature at university before deciding on gardening as a career. His extensive practical gardening experience has included a period of six years working as head gardener to the late J.B. Priestley. For some years the gardening correspondent for *The Field*, he is now a regular contributor to *Homes & Gardens* and other publications. Author of *Topiary* and *The Integrated Garden*, he combines writing with the restoration of a large traditional kitchen garden at his home near Stratford-upon-Avon, Warwickshire.